DUBLIN
AND HER PEOPLE

Published in Ireland by
Gill and Macmillan Ltd
Goldenbridge
Dublin 8
with associated companies in
Auckland, Dallas, Delhi, Hong Kong,
Johannesburg, Lagos, London, Manzini,
Melbourne, Nairobi, New York, Singapore,
Tokyo, Washington
© Photographs, 1991, Colour Library Books Ltd, Godalming,
    Surrey, England
© Text, 1991, Gill and Macmillan Ltd
Printed in Singapore
ISBN 0 7171 1864 9

DUBLIN
AND HER PEOPLE

Gill and Macmillan

An old popular song tells us that 'Dublin can be heaven…'. Ireland's capital has always had a special atmosphere. The pace of life is slower than that of London or Paris or New York, but this is still recognisably a great capital city, full of presence and personality.

Dublin began life as a convenient place for fording the River Liffey and as such it was used by Celtic tribesmen in ancient Ireland. But the Celts were not town-dwellers and it was not until the arrival of the Vikings in the early ninth century A.D. that the first permanent settlement was established. This was on the rising ground on the south bank of the river in the area where Christ Church Cathedral is today.

Following the Vikings came the Anglo-Normans. They too concentrated their attention in the Christ Church area. In 1204, they began work on Dublin Castle which, although it has undergone many changes since, was for over 700 years the centre of British power in Ireland. Even today, the real powers in the land still occupy Dublin Castle in the form of the Revenue Commissioners, the collectors of Ireland's income taxes!

Very little survives of medieval Dublin. The two cathedrals – Christ Church and St Patrick's – had fallen into decay by the late nineteenth century and were both heavily renovated and restored at that time. Just to show that the manufacture of alcoholic drink has always been a profitable enterprise in. Dublin, the money for the Christ Church restoration was contributed by a distiller, Henry Roe, and that for St Patrick's by a brewer, Benjamin Lee Guinness!

By the late seventeenth century, Dublin was in a sorry state. It had few buildings of distinction and was altogether a rather shabby and impoverished place. Then it entered on its golden age. In a great burst of energy and creativity, Georgian Dublin was built. To this day, it is the eighteenth-century city that is the essential Dublin. The great public buildings which still adorn the city – the Royal Hospital, the old Bank of Ireland, Trinity College west front, the Custom House, City Hall, the Rotunda Hospital, the Municipal Art Gallery, the General Post Office, Leinster House, the Four Courts and the King's Inns – were all built between 1685 and 1820.

In addition, this brilliant period also saw the development of the great squares and Georgian streets on both sides of the river which still give central Dublin its distinctive character. A Wide Streets Commission was established in the 1750s to oversee all this development and the fruits of their wise work are still to be seen, especially in the gracious streets of the inner south city. Stand, for instance, at the corner of Merrion Square West and Merrion Street with your back to Leinster House and look down along the south side of the square and into Upper Mount Street. The vista is closed off by the beautiful St Stephen's Church at the end of that street, known to everyone in Dublin as the Peppercanister Church. This is as elegant and charming a streetscape as can be found anywhere in Europe.

The Act of Union of 1801, which abolished the old Irish Parliament and brought Ireland wholly under the control of London, ushered in a long period of decline. Some of the great Georgian buildings fell into decay, particularly on the north side of the city, as many of the resident aristocracy moved to England. None the less, Victorian Dublin expanded with the coming of the railways and in many ways, the suburbs that were built at that time are as typical of the city as anything from the Georgian period.

Modern Dublin has expanded too, especially in the past twenty years or so. And while not all the new buildings are to everyone's taste, there are, nevertheless, some very fine examples of contemporary architecture to be found in the city.

But a city is more than buildings. Most of all, it is people. And Dubliners are as well known as ever for their wit, their conversation and their good humour. Of course, it helps to live in a city by the sea, with the beautiful hills and mountains of Co. Wicklow just to the south. So you should do the things that Dubliners do: take a walk in the Phoenix Park, spend a little time (or a lot of time) in some of the best pubs in the world, go to the races at Leopardstown or to Croke Park to see hurling and Gaelic football, or just stroll around one of the old streets and soak up the atmosphere. It's true what they say: 'Dublin can be heaven…'.

Left: the rectangular layout of Dublin's Trinity College beside the semi-circular façade of the Bank of Ireland.
Previous pages: O'Connell Bridge and Street.

An imposing statue of Daniel O'Connell (*above*), by sculptor John Henry Foley, dominates the southern end of O'Connell Street, Dublin's principal thoroughfare and one of the broadest streets in Europe. In the 1740s Luke Gardiner, whose family did much to beautify the city, widened the street to 150 feet and planted the mall with trees, and it became one of the first areas to constitute the fashionable north Dublin of the 18th century. *Facing page*: the splendid Renaissance-style building in Kildare Street that became the home of the National Library in 1890, (*right*) Heuston Station, a striking building designed by Sancton Wood and dating from the mid-1840s, and (*above right*) Leinster House, which was built in 1745 and is one of the finest of Dublin's Georgian mansions. Originally the town house of the Dukes of Leinster, it became Government property in the early 1900s, providing accommodation for the two houses of the Republic of Ireland Parliament.

GEORGE BERNARD SHAW
1856-1950

Standing in elegant Merrion Square is an institution of which Dubliners are particularly proud, the National Gallery of Ireland (*these pages*). It was opened in 1864 largely due to the efforts of William Dargan, the prime instigator of the Exhibition of 1853. A statue of him stands outside the building (*below*), as does a statue of George Bernard Shaw (*facing page bottom left*), who maintained that he owed his education to the gallery and left a third of his estate to it. Designed by Francis Fowke, the gallery has some fine rooms in which is housed a remarkable collection including works from all major European schools and a comprehensive selection from Irish artists. *Overleaf*: the decorative stairwells of (*left*) the National Gallery and (*right*) City Hall.

Built by Francis Johnston in 1815-18, the General Post Office (*above*), on O'Connell Street, is an impressive building and is also of historic interest, having been the headquarters of the Irish Volunteers during the Insurrection of 1916. Its interior was badly damaged by shells but has since been restored to its original splendour and features a plaque (*right*) bearing the declaration of the patriots. *Facing page*: the Four Courts (*top*), overlooking the River Liffey, has housed Dublin's Courts of Law since 1796, when they were moved there from the precincts of Christ Church Cathedral. The six Corinthian columns of the portico are surmounted by a statue of Moses, with Justice and Mercy on either side. The Bank of Ireland (*bottom*), one of the finest Georgian buildings in the city, was begun by Edward Lovett Pearce in 1729. Statues depicting Hibernia, Fidelity and Commerce stand above the elegant Ionic portico.

"WE DECLARE THE RIGHT OF THE PEOPLE OF IRELAND TO THE OWNERSHIP OF IRELAND. AND TO THE UNFETTERED CONTROL OF IRISH DESTINIES, TO BE SOVEREIGN AND INDEFEASIBLE. THE LONG USURPATION OF THAT RIGHT BY A FOREIGN PEOPLE AND GOVERNMENT HAS NOT EXTINGUISHED THE RIGHT, NOR CAN IT EVER BE EXTINGUISHED EXCEPT BY THE DESTRUCTION OF THE IRISH PEOPLE. IN EVERY GENERATION THE IRISH PEOPLE HAVE ASSERTED THEIR RIGHT TO NATIONAL FREEDOM AND SOVEREIGNTY: SIX TIMES DURING THE PAST THREE HUNDRED YEARS THEY HAVE ASSERTED IT IN ARMS. STANDING ON THAT FUNDAMENTAL RIGHT AND AGAIN ASSERTING IT IN ARMS IN THE FACE OF THE WORLD. WE HEREBY PROCLAIM THE IRISH REPUBLIC AS A SOVEREIGN INDEPENDENT STATE. AND WE PLEDGE OUR LIVES AND THE LIVES OF OUR COMRADES-IN-ARMS TO THE CAUSE OF ITS FREEDOM, OF ITS WELFARE, AND OF ITS EXALTATION AMONG THE NATIONS."

THOMAS J. CLARKE.

SEAN MacDIARMADA,   THOMAS MacDONAGH.

P. H. PEARSE,   EAMONN CEANNT.

JAMES CONNOLLY,   JOSEPH PLUNKETT.

Previous pages: a view of the River Liffey at sunset. Rising near Sally Gap in the Wicklow Hills, the river describes almost a full circle as it flows eastwards into Dublin's harbour, emptying into the sea at Dublin Bay. Marsh's Library (*these pages*), on the east side of St Patrick's Cathedral, was built by Archbishop Narcissus Marsh in 1707 and is the oldest of Ireland's public libraries. Its darkened oak shelves contain some 25,000 beautifully-bound volumes – chiefly of medicine, theology and ancient literature – and its treasures include Dean Swift's copy of Clarendon's "History of the Great Rebellion" with his own pencilled annotations. *Overleaf*: a view of broad O'Connell Street from the south side of O'Connell Bridge.

Facing page: (*top*) elegant Georgian houses on Merrion Square, and (*bottom*) Leinster House and the cenotaph to Arthur Griffith and Michael Collins. *Right*: a statue of Robert Emmet in St Stephen's Green (*this page*), where many Dubliners choose to relax.

The 1980s witnessed many changes in city centre shopping in Dublin. New, purpose-built shopping centres and re-developments of existing premises combined to give the shopper a much wider variety of choice. St Stephen's Green Shopping Centre (*left*) opened towards the end of the decade. Situated on the north-west corner of the Green, the clever use of glass in its design gives a light, airy feeling inside the centre (*below*). The Westbury Mall (*right*) is a much smaller development. Adjacent to the Westbury Hotel, it provides an attractive range of small shops. The Powerscourt Town House Centre (*below right and overleaf*) was built in 1771 to the design of Robert Mack who had previously designed Grattan Bridge linking Capel Street and Parliament Street. Located on South William Street, Powerscourt Town House Centre was once owned by a wholesale textile firm; it was re-opened in the early 1980s as a shopping mall.

Facing page bottom: looking seawards down the River Liffey with the Metal Footbridge – or Halfpenny Bridge – in the foreground. Further downstream Liberty Hall dominates the left bank while the domed Custom House looms on the horizon.
Facing page top: Queen Maeve Bridge leading to Arran Quay, which is dominated by the tower of St Paul's Church, dating from 1835-40. Beyond is the green dome of the Four Courts, which rises above the jostling roofs of quayside houses (*below*). O'Connell Bridge (*right*) leads into O'Connell Street and was first named Carlisle Bridge when it was built in 1794. In 1880 it was renamed, flattened and widened, making it rather remarkable in that it is now broader than it is long. The magnificent reading room (*overleaf*) in the National Library was opened in 1890 to house the collections of the Royal Dublin Society, previously housed at Leinster House.

Christic Church Cathedral (*these pages*) is Dublin's oldest building, having been founded by Donat, first Bishop of Dublin, and the Norse King Sitric of Dublin in about 1038. In 1172 construction was renewed on a greater scale with the help of sponsorship from Strongbow and St Laurence O'Toole. Its splendid interior contains some fascinating treasures, including an effigy of Strongbow (*below right*), supposedly marking his burial place, with another alongside said to be either that of his wife or of his son, whom according to legend he cut in two for being a coward. Exquisite chandeliers light the sumptuous Drawing Room (*overleaf*) of the State Apartments in Dublin Castle. Originally a Norse stronghold dating from 1208 to 1220, the castle proper was built during the reign of King John, eventually becoming the residence of the lord deputy, or viceroy.

This page: views of the River Liffey at dusk, spanned by O'Connell Bridge (*facing page top*), Queen Maeve Bridge (*right*) and the famous Metal Footbridge (*remaining pictures*), which was built in 1816 and is also known as Halfpenny Bridge due to the toll charged in the early 1900s. Flowing from the west to Dublin Bay in the east, the River Liffey cuts through the very heart of Dublin, and a walk along its banks can be a good way to become acquainted with aspects of the city's character. Lining the busy quays are to be found warehouses, the variously-painted façades of tenement buildings and auction rooms full of odds and ends, as well as some of the city's finest buildings.

The friendliness of Dublin's vendors makes shopping there a very pleasurable experience, especially at lively markets such as those in Thomas Street (*above and facing page bottom*) and St Michans's Street (*right and top pictures*). *Facing page top*: shops on Meath Street.

Apart from its merit as an educational establishment, Trinity College (*these pages*) has a long and prestigious history, having been founded by Elizabeth I in 1592. Being situated at the centre of Ireland's capital it has played a greater role in the country's affairs than is usual for a university, and has often been a forum for heated political debate. An impressive number of great minds have flourished in its lively atmosphere – Congreve, Bishop Berkeley, Swift, Emmet and Wilde to name but a few. The college's spacious quadrangle is dominated by the Campanile (*below and facing page bottom*), which was built by Sir Charles Lanyon in 1853, while its grand, Palladian-style West Front (*remaining pictures*) was built between 1752 and 1759. *Overleaf*: O'Connell Street and O'Connell Bridge.

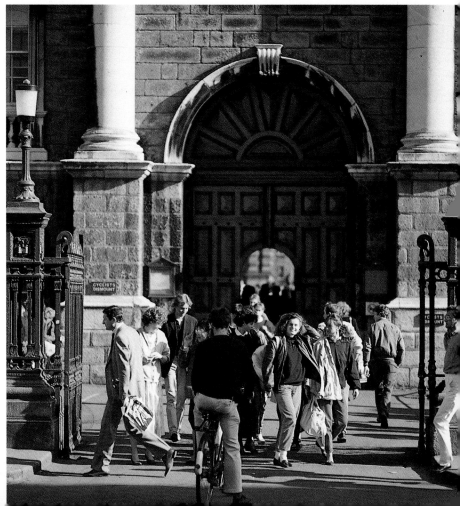

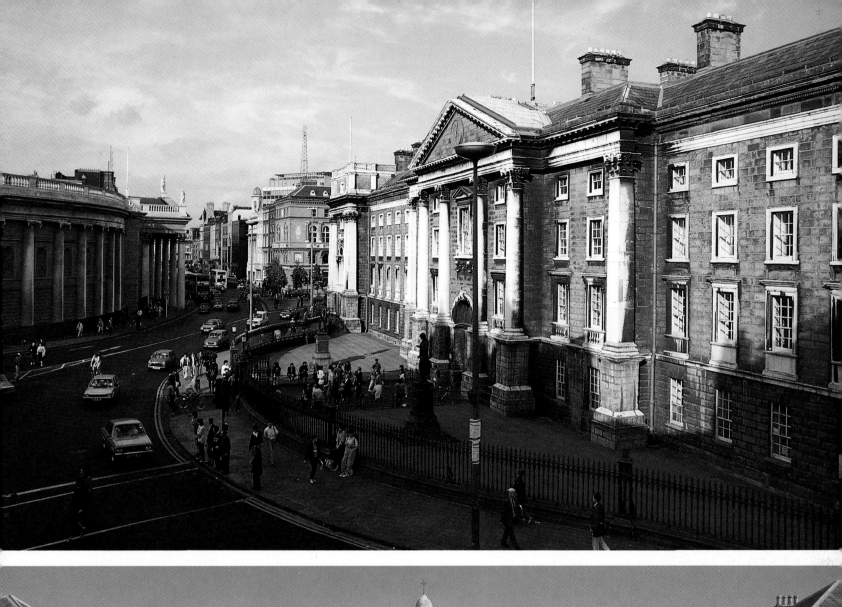

Facing page: animals at Dublin Zoo, which was established in 1830 and is the world's third oldest public zoo. It is among the many attractions in Phoenix Park (*remaining pictures*), which, covering around 2,000 acres, is one of Europe's largest parks.

Previous pages: (*left*) Government Buildings, formerly the Science Buildings of University College, designed by Sir Aston Webb, R.A. and built in 1904-10, and (*right*) the President of Ireland's residence, built in the 1750s by Nathaniel Clements and set in the green expanse of Phoenix Park. The city centre has seen many changes in recent years. Two major multi-million pound developments have opened in recent times. The St Stephen's Green Shopping Centre (*below*) contains more than 100 different shopping units, providing a wide variety for shoppers in a pleasant, airy environment. 1990 saw the opening of Dublin's Financial Services Centre (*right and left*). Built on long disused land adjacent to Dublin docks, it provided a much-needed boost to the north-east side of the city.

The village of Malahide, a resort on the coast north of Dublin, is distinguished by its fine castle (*previous pages*), the residence of the Talbot de Malahide family from 1185 to 1976. Set in 265 acres of land, it comprises buildings from several periods, including the 12th-century, three storey tower house and two drum-like towers dating from around 1765. Among the treasures within the castle is a fine collection of portraits forming the nucleus of the National Gallery's National Portrait Collection. It includes a number of portrayals of people and events relevant to the castle's and Ireland's history. Along with many fine Georgian buildings, the streets of central Dublin are enhanced by the traditional façades of its shops, pubs and theatres (*these pages*), whose colourful paintwork and ornate signs bring to mind an age gone by. *Left*: the Olympia Theatre on Dame Street, and (*below*) the Brazen Head Hotel, which has a bar that is reputedly the city's oldest, dating from 1666.

Situated near the main south-east gate of Phoenix Park is a striking, 205-feet-high obelisk, the Wellington Testimonial (*facing page*), which was erected two years after Waterloo, in 1817. Designed by Sir William Smirke, its pedestal is decorated with bronze panels depicting Wellington's battles in bas relief. On the south bank of the River Liffey, near Kilmainham, is Memorial Park (*right*), which was laid out by Lutyens and commemorates the First World War. *Below*: the smooth waters of the Liffey under a golden sky, dominated by the Wellington Testimonial.

The National Museum was designed in Renaissance style by Sir Thomas Deane and opened in 1890. Its exquisitely decorated interior (*previous pages*) contains a large collection of Irish antiquities dating from the Stone Age period onwards. Some of the most beautiful of its priceless exhibits are the gold pieces of jewellery from the Bronze Age, while other items include the Ardagh Chalice and the Tara Brooch, both dating from the eighth century. *Above*: the grand entrance to Government Buildings, formerly the Science Buildings of University College, and (*left*) the Campanile in the quadrangle of Trinity College, which is also the site of the 'Long Room' (*facing page*). This beautiful library measures 209 feet in length and houses some of the finest Celtic manuscripts in the world, including the Book of Durrow and the Book of Kells.

Left: the covered market off Great George's Street, (*below and bottom left*) Greene's Bookshop in Clare Street, (*bottom*) Merchant's Alley, and (*facing page*) the Parnell Monument at the northern end of O'Connell Street. *Overleaf*: Parnell Street.

TO
CHARLES STEWART PARNELL

"NO·MAN·HAS·A·RIGHT·TO·FIX·THE·
BOUNDARY·TO·THE·MARCH·OF·A·NATION·
NO·MAN·HAS·A·RIGHT·
TO·SAY·TO·HIS·COUNTRY·
THUS·FAR·SHALT·THOU·
GO·AND·NO·FURTHER·
WE·HAVE·NEVER·
ATTEMPTED·TO·FIX·
THE·NE·PLUS·ULTRA·
TO·THE·PROGRESS·OF·
IRELANDS·NATIONHOOD·
AND·WE·NEVER·SHALL"·

ʒo·roinbiʒió·ória
éine·óá·clainn

Facing page: (*top*) the Nissan Bicycle Race and (*bottom*) the Dublin Marathon. *Top*: the Four Courts, overlooking the River Liffey, and (*above*) the interior and (*right*) gate of the Tailors Hall, which dates from 1796 and is the city's only remaining guild hall.

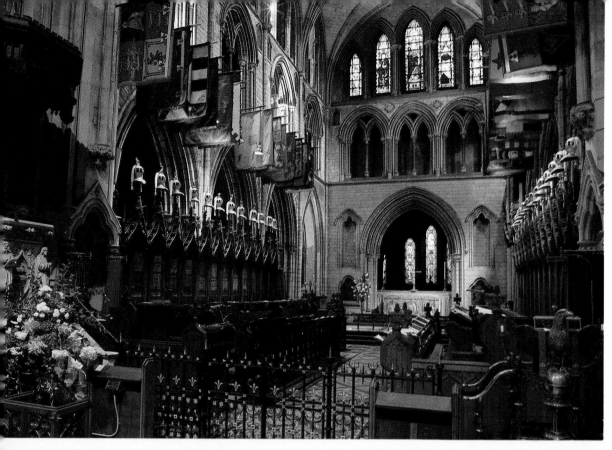

According to tradition, St Patrick's Cathedral (*these pages*) stands where the saint himself baptised converts in a well that appeared when he struck the ground with his staff. The original church dates from 1192 yet the present magnificent edifice – at 300 feet, the longest church in Ireland – is largely the result of restoration carried out in the 19th century. Of particular interest is the church's association with the celebrated, and bitter, satirist Jonathan Swift, who was Dean of St Patrick's from 1713 to 1745. He is buried in the south aisle, where – according to the epitaph he wrote himself – "savage indignation can no longer rend his heart". The Four Courts (*overleaf*), on the north bank of the River Liffey, was built between 1786 and 1802 by the great architect, James Gandon. It contains the original courts of Exchequer, Common Pleas, King's Bench and Chancery.

Facing page: fruit and vegetable stalls on Moore Street, and colourful flowers on sale at the market (*top*) in the arcade between Great George's Street and Drury Street and (*above and left*) in Grafton Street. *Overleaf*: the O'Connell Monument on O'Connell Street.

Left: the formidable gates of Kilmainham Jail (*remaining pictures*), which dates from 1792 and has lodged such famous Irish patriots as Parnell, Davitt and Robert Emmet. It was also the execution place of many Volunteer leaders, including Patrick Pearse and James Connolly, and is now open as a museum.

When it was begun in 1729 the Bank of Ireland (*above*) was intended to house the Irish Parliament. It was, however, made redundant in 1800 when the British and Irish parliaments united in London under the Act of Union. When the building was sold, for the sum of £40,000, it was stipulated that the interior should be redesigned so as to exclude its use as a public debating forum. The only room to retain its original appearance is the Old House of Lords (*right*), in which is hung a splendid 1,233-piece, Waterford crystal chandelier and two great tapestries woven by Jan van Beaver depicting the Battle of the Boyne and the Siege of Derry. *Facing page:* (*top*) O'Connell Bridge, and (*bottom*) Heuston Bridge and Station. *Overleaf:* aerial views of central Dublin, picturing (*left*) the curving façade of the Bank of Ireland and Westmoreland Street leading over the Liffey into O'Connell Street, and (*right*) the domed Four Courts, the square tower of Christ Church Cathedral and the quadrangle and crenellated Record Tower of Dublin Castle.

One of Dublin's most prized assets is Phoenix Park (*these pages*), which first belonged to the priory of the Knights of St John, was seized by Henry VIII at the Reformation and was opened to the public in the mid-1700s by the viceroy, Lord Chesterfield. Amongst its many interesting sights is the towering cross of steel (*facing page*) that stands where Pope John Paul II celebrated mass during his visit in 1979. *Overleaf*: the market on Moore Street.

Top: the control room, (*top left and left*) the exhibition at the Malt House, and (*above*) the gates, of the Guinness Brewery (*facing page*), where the famed Dublin stout has been made since 1759. *Overleaf*: the Royal Hospital in Kilmainham, with its ornate chapel (*right*).

Top and left: the fine building that was once the Canal Hotel, at Portobello Lock and Canal (*above*). Facing page: (*top*) the Mansion House, where the lord mayors of Dublin have lived since 1715, and (*bottom*) Leinster House, built in 1745.

One of the most macabre of the city's historic sights is the group of mummified bodies (*previous pages left*) in the crypt of St Michan's Church. It is likely that their extraordinary preservation is due to the moisture-absorbing power of the church's limestone walls, although a more imaginative explanation attributes it to the embalming spirit released in an explosion at a nearby distillery. St Michan's is one of Dublin's oldest churches, having been founded in 1095, though much of the present edifice is the result of 17th-century rebuilding and 19th-century restoration. Among its many points of interest is the old organ in the main aisle (*previous pages, right*) that was reputedly played by Handel. *Right*: St Audoen's Church, which is the city's earliest existing parish church, dating mainly from the 12th century, (*below*) the Royal Hospital, founded by Charles II and built in 1680-84 for veteran and disabled soldiers, and (*below right*) a memorial stone backed by Collins Barracks, formerly the Royal Barracks of 1704. *Facing page*: a lock on the Grand Canal.

Previous pages: colourful clothes and bric-à-brac in Iveagh Markets, in Francis Street. Located within easy reach of the city centre is a variety of picturesque and interesting places to visit. Running parallel to the northern shores of Dublin Bay is the three-mile-long sandbank, North Bull Island, which in days gone by was the cause of countless shipwrecks, providing local residents with great quantities of booty. Today, the island's attractions include long stretches of golden beach (*facing page bottom*), a bird sanctuary and two golf courses. Further east, crowning the bay's northern arm, is beautiful Howth Head (*remaining pictures*). A splendid 15th-century castle can be seen from the road leading to charming Howth Village, which is known for its beautiful gardens and great, sheltered harbour (*facing page top*). The latter, built in 1807-9, is used as a fishing port as well as a mooring place for pleasure craft (*right*). From 19th-century Baily Lighthouse (*above*), on the southern shores of Howth Head, the Wicklow Hills are visible. *Overleaf*: Halfpenny Bridge and the lights of Dublin reflected in the River Liffey.